This Book Belong to:

_____

Content

Piano Sonata No.10 in C major, K.330/300h.........3

Piano Sonata No.11 in A major, K.331/300i.........21

Piano Sonata No.12 in F major, K.332/300k..........40

Piano Sonata No.13 in B-flat major, K.333/315c..61

Piano Sonata No.14 in C minor, K.457...................82

Piano Sonata No.15 in F major, K.533/494.........101

Piano Sonata No.16 in C major, K.545..................122

Piano Sonata No.17 in B-flat major, K.570..........133

Piano Sonata No.18 in D major, K.576............... 146

Piano Sonata No.10 in C major, K.330/300h

SONATE

Köchel Nr. 330

Allegro moderato

Andante cantabile

*) Erstausgabe von Artaria (1784). Autograph ohne Coda / First print by Artaria (1784). Autograph without Coda
Première édition d'Artaria (1784). Autographe sans Coda

19

Piano Sonata No.11 in A major, K.331/300i

SONATE

W. A. Mozart
Köchel Nr. 331

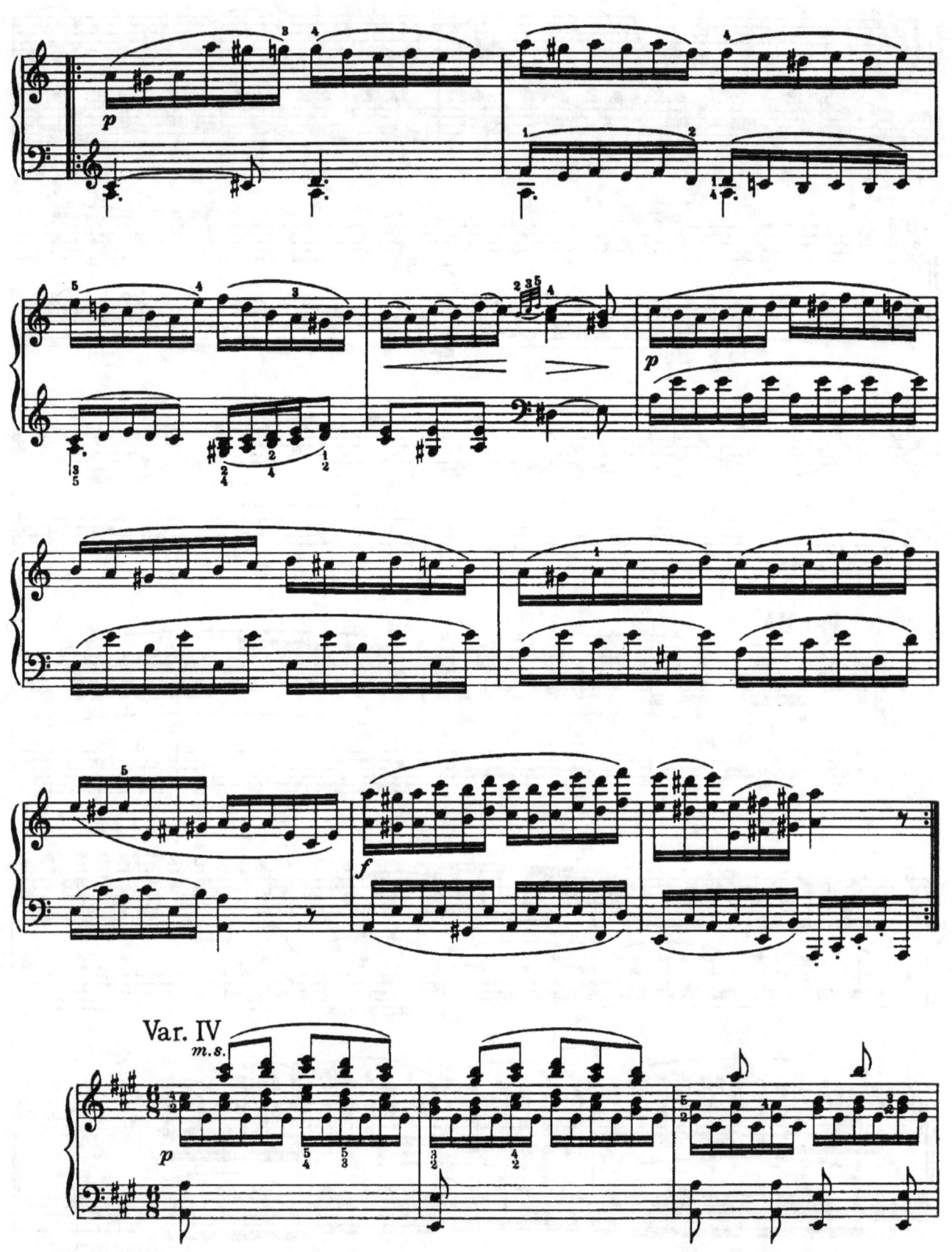

Var. VI
Allegro

Alla turca
Allegretto

35

Coda

Piano Sonata No.12 in F major, K.332/300k

SONATE

Köchel Nr. 332

43

45

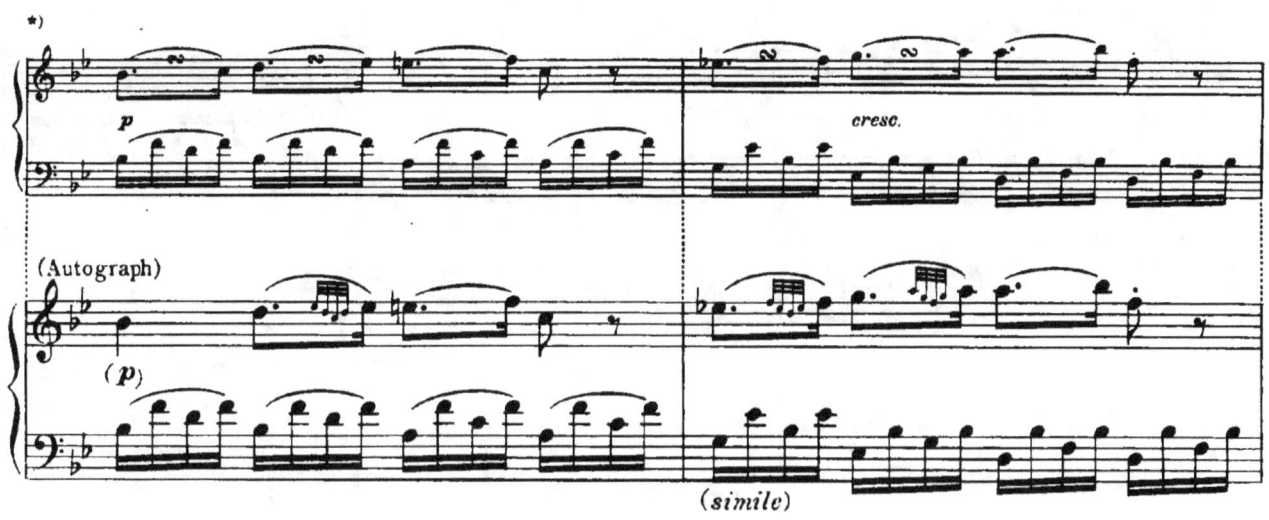

(Autograph)

*) Lesart der ältesten Drucke   *Reading of the earliest prints*   Version des éditions les plus anciennes

Assai Allegro

Piano Sonata No.13 in B-flat major, K.333/315c

SONATE

Allegro

Köchel Nr. 333

Piano Sonata No.14 in C minor, K.457

SONATE

Köchel Nr. 457

Molto Allegro

*) Autograph. In der Erstausgabe von Artaria (1785) fehlen die Verzierungen | In the first print by Artaria (1785) the embellishments are missing | Dans la première édition d'Artaria (1785) les ornements sont omis

*) Artaria (1785). Autograph:

Allegro assai

*) Artaria. Das Autograph enthält die folgende (kühnere) Fassung dieser acht Takte, die Mozart zweifellos selbst für den Druck änderte:

Artaria. The autograph contains the following (more venturous) version of these eight measures which, no doubt, Mozart himself changed for the print:

Artaria. L'autographe contient de ces huit mesures la version (plus hardie) que voici laquelle, à n'en pas douter, Mozart lui-même a changée pour l'impression:

Piano Sonata No.15 in F major, K.533/494

SONATE

Köchel Nr. 533

Piano Sonata No.16 in C major, K.545

SONATA FACILE

Köchel Nr. 545

Rondo
Allegretto

Piano Sonata No.17 in B-flat major, K.570

SONATE N.º 17
für das Pianoforte
von
W. A. MOZART.
Köch.Verz. N.º 576.

Componirt Juli 1789 in Wien.

W. A. M. 576.

139

Piano Sonata No.18 in D major, K.576

SONATE

Köchel Nr. 570

147

www.ingramcontent.com/pod-product-compliance
Lightning Source LLC
Chambersburg PA
CBHW081618100526
44590CB00021B/3493